T0328875

JEREMIAH

THE PROPHET OF HOPE

JEREMIAH

THE PROPHET OF HOPE

BY

DOROTHEA STEPHEN, S.Th.

AUTHOR OF
STUDIES IN EARLY INDIAN THOUGHT

CAMBRIDGE
AT THE UNIVERSITY PRESS
1923

TO

THE MEMBERS

OF THE

IRISH GUILD OF WITNESS

CAMBRIDGE
UNIVERSITY PRESS

University Printing House, Cambridge CB2 8BS, United Kingdom

Cambridge University Press is part of the University of Cambridge.

It furthers the University's mission by disseminating knowledge in the pursuit of education, learning and research at the highest international levels of excellence.

www.cambridge.org
Information on this title: www.cambridge.org/9781316509579

© Cambridge University Press 1923

First published 1923
First paperback edition 2015

A catalogue record for this publication is available from the British Library

ISBN 978-1-316-50957-9 Paperback

PREFACE

IN days when hope is not a sentiment but a task and an adventure, the story of Jeremiah has a new value for us. This little book makes no pretence to detailed criticism or wide research; it is meant only to help the general reader to a clearer understanding of what that value is and it requires the study of no book except the Bible itself.

D. J. STEPHEN.

30 *Nov.* 1921.

CONTENTS

JEREMIAH THE PROPHET
OF HOPE

CHAPTER I

FIRST PERIOD 626–608 B.C.

THE REIGN OF JOSIAH

THERE were several occasions in the history of Judah when the worship of Yahweh was reasserted in the face of idolatry and a reformation carried out in the name of the reigning sovereign. Asa removed the sodomites and the idols[1]; Jehoshaphat removed the sodomites[2]; the priest Jehoiada, acting for the infant Jehoash, broke the images of Baal and killed his priest[3], and though no actual reformation is mentioned in the reigns of Uzziah and his son Jotham, both are specially said to have been good kings[4], but we find that, neither by them nor by their predecessors was anything done to remove the High Places all over the country where the people still sacrificed and burnt incense, as indeed their fathers had always done, the Judges, Samuel and, in later days, Elijah[5].

---

[1] I Kings xv. 12.   [2] *Ib.* xxii. 46.
[3] II Kings xi. 18.   [4] *Ib.* xv. 3, 34.
[5] I Kings xxii. 43; II Kings xii. 3, xv. 4, 35.

This worship at the High Places was, in fact, a very ancient practice and was in accordance with the law given in the Book of the Covenant, that an altar shall be built in every place where the Lord 'recorded his name' or 'caused it to be remembered[1]'; but as time passed the feeling of the best part of the nation turned against it because of the corruption that seemed to be inseparable from it. We have a vivid picture of what that corruption was in the writings of Hosea[2], and we may see the same thing in our own day in any country where people use stones or posts as emblems of fertility, as many do. But though this worship might become gross and corrupt, it was not apostate in the eyes of the worshippers of Yahweh, who was adored under the form of Baal, the Lord of the soil, and the giver of the fruits of the earth. When Rabshakeh came on behalf of Sennacherib in 701 B.C., he reminded the people of this; it was, he said, the High Places of the Lord that Hezekiah had taken away, and it was the Lord who had sent the Assyrians to avenge the sacrilege[3].

Hezekiah was, in fact, the first king of Judah who removed the High Places; he broke the 'pillars,' the upright stones representing Baal, and cut down the Asherah, the wooden posts that

---

[1] Ex. xx. 24.   [2] Hosea ii.   [3] II Kings xviii. 22.

accompanied them, and his action marked a new stage in the development of the religion of Israel[1]. Old customs die hard and there may have been those among the men on the wall who listened to Rabshakeh who feared that he might be right, and that Yahweh was indeed offended; but they were silent, and soon the destruction of Sennacherib's army, followed by the deliverance of Jerusalem, justified the king before the people.

But Hezekiah's reformation did not survive him; under his son Manasseh, all his work was swept away. For fifty-five years the High Places were restored, Yahweh's presence and blessing were sought in them with the ancient rites, the reformers of Hezekiah's time were persecuted and killed, and not only so, but new forms of worship were introduced; the Queen of Heaven, the great goddess of Assyria and all Western Asia, was worshipped by each family on the house roofs, and Moloch, the great Baal of Tyre, received offerings of children in the valley of Topheth; the king himself sacrificed his son in the fire as his grandfather Ahaz had done before him[2].

It was towards the end of this reign that Jeremiah was born.

Our knowledge of Jeremiah comes chiefly from the book which bears his name; there is no mention

[1] II Kings xviii. 1–4.   [2] Ib. xxi. 6, xvi. 3.

of him in the book of Kings and none in Chronicles till the last chapter, where we are told that he lamented over Josiah and advised Zedekiah in vain. But happily his oracles have been carefully preserved from the first, both by himself and later by his friends and disciples. We have the full account of how he came to collect all his earlier teaching in a book, and how, when that book was destroyed, he wrote it again and added to it[1]. The book of Jeremiah itself, as a complete whole with the introduction and explanatory verses, and the occasional historical accounts of events, seems to be the work of his friend and secretary, Baruch. The actual oracles, poems and addresses have been preserved, but not arranged, as we might perhaps have wished they had been, in chronological order, so as to give a consecutive history; they have been grouped according to subject, and if we want to reconstruct the history, we shall have to rearrange the oracles. One of the chief of these groups consists of the oracles on foreign nations, which have been put together at the end of the book[2] and, valuable as they are, we shall have to follow the example of the original editor, and leave them on one side, so as to confine ourselves to the history of Judah. As actually spoken they were a continual witness to Jeremiah's belief that Yahweh

---

[1] Jer. xxxvi.   [2] *Ib.* xlvi to li.

was the Lord not of Judah only, but of all the world. The oracles on the last four kings of Judah form another group[1]. Jehoahaz, Jehoiachim, Jehoiachin and probably Zedekiah are all described and judgment passed on their doings. In one place two oracles are put side by side, apparently because in each of them an earthen bottle is mentioned[2]; in another place because both are about conspiracies, the one about the conspiracy against the Lord in Jerusalem, the other about a conspiracy against Jeremiah in Anathoth[3]. The Jews did not care much for the critical study of documents; it seemed to them enough to know that these various oracles had been spoken by the Lord, or by his mouthpiece the prophet; we have learnt by long experience to see that there is value, not only in the actual word, but also in its setting of time and circumstance. It will therefore be our task to take the jewels from the pile one by one and try to place them in their original order; it is often impossible to do this with absolute certainty. Some of the oracles are dated and these will give us something to start from; as for the rest, scholars will never agree in every particular, but the general outline will be clear, and our object will have been gained if we can so arrange our material as to gain a coherent view of Jeremiah's thought, of what it was for

[1] Jer. xxii, xxiii.   [2] *Ib.* xviii, xix.   [3] *Ib.* xi. 9–14, 18–23.

which he and his friends lived and fought, and of how far they failed or succeeded. If the oracles are read according to the order suggested in the lists at the end of each chapter, it will be found that a coherent picture of the prophet's life presents itself.

We shall find that a certain number of passages are, by this detailed study, removed altogether from the time of Jeremiah and must be supposed to be from some other writer. For instance in one place, where Jeremiah himself has been speaking, there is a slight change of subject and he is suddenly referred to in the third person; evidently some later writer is enlarging on what he has said. We must judge of such passages as they occur[1].

Jeremiah was a descendant of Abiathar the priest, who had been exiled from Jerusalem to Anathoth by Solomon, while his successful rival, Zadok, stayed at court. The rivalry between Abiathar and Zadok was an old one, we can trace it in the story of David's life. The writer of the book of Samuel tells us that the family of Abiathar lay under a curse, for the weakness of Eli and the wickedness of his sons, and that they should come to beg work of their successors so as to earn a piece of bread[2]; but it is not very likely that this was the tradition preserved among themselves. In the

[1] Jer. xxv. 12–14.   [2] I Sam. ii. 27–36, iii. 11–14.

reign of David, they were the king's friends and on an equality with the Zadokites, but, after his death, they took the wrong side in the dispute between his sons, and fell in the fall of Adonijah[1]. We cannot tell whether, when Jeremiah was a child, they still carried on the worship at the High Place of Anathoth; no doubt this was one of the High Places destroyed by Hezekiah, for it was only four miles from Jerusalem. They would have been free to restore it if they chose in the reign of Manasseh, and may conceivably have done so feeling that Yahweh would be better served there than in the desecrated Temple in the capital; or, again, they may have been among those who believed that the corruption of these country sanctuaries made their destruction necessary, and in this case they must have lived for a generation without public worship, and have been glad to escape with their lives from a king who massacred his subjects and burnt his son at Topheth[2].

While Jeremiah was still a child, Manasseh died, and was succeeded by his son Amon, who followed in his steps for two years, and was then murdered; but with the next king came a change. He too was a child, and those who had charge of him were of a very different temper from his father and grandfather. They began doing or

[1] I Kings ii. 26–27.　　[2] II Kings xxi. 6.

making him do 'that which was right in the eyes of the Lord,' and at least the terrors of Manasseh's reign were over. The book of Chronicles, which was written much later, after the Exile and the Return, gives a detailed report of his reforming activity in the early part of his reign, before his eighteenth year, but nothing is said of this in the book of Kings[1]. At any rate this eighteenth year marked a turning point in his policy.

Meanwhile, Jeremiah was growing up to be a young man, gradually realising the trouble of the times and of the society round him. His mind dwelt on the dream of a bygone golden age of primitive simplicity, when people were poor and lived by their flocks and herds, and on the water and manna miraculously given them in the Wilderness, before they had begun to plant corn and vines or to look to the Baalim for the gifts of the fertile earth. In the thirteenth year of the reign came his call to be a prophet, a destroyer and a restorer to all nations.

Through all Jeremiah's life there is nothing abnormal, he works no wonder, he tells no dream and sees no vision, except for such simple images as might suggest themselves to anyone whether in actual outward fact or in inward fancy, a branch of almond tree, a boiling pot, two baskets of figs.

[1] II Chron. xxxiv. 1–7; II Kings xxii. 1, 2.

In the account of his call the celestial imagery that surrounded the call of Isaiah is not there. The voice that speaks to him is, as far as we are told, inward, such as any man may hear. Nor does Jeremiah offer himself, as Isaiah did; on the contrary he shrinks and only obeys a direct command. His lips are touched, not by a coal in the hands of a seraph, not by fire from the altar, but by the hand of the Lord. The only miracle he knows is the presence of God and that is constant. Indeed, for anyone who could not see that, there was no other sign to be given in his time.

The thirteenth year of Josiah was 626 B.C., and this was the period of the Scythian invasions. Wild tribes of barbarians came from the north and raided the Assyrian empire, now grown feeble. Judah was still a province of that empire, but there was no longer any protection to be had from Nineveh. The Scythians broke out from Central Asia, driven probably by famine in their own countries, bringing fire and sword, ravaging all the rich lands within their reach and then vanishing again into the deserts beyond the known world. This disaster on such a scale was a new thing in the history of the civilised nations of the world. Robber incursions were common enough, like those of the Midianites or Philistines, who invaded Israel in the time of the Judges, or of Israel itself when it conquered Canaan; but these Northern barbarians were different. They were of an unknown race and from an unknown country and they attacked not only one city or state but the whole world. Nineveh itself, the capital of the empire, could not turn them back, the terrible armies that Isaiah had described with their arrows and horses and chariots roaring like lions put no barrier in their way[1]. The new invasion seemed to be the end of the world. Zephaniah calls it the day of wrath, and the expectation of it colours Jeremiah's first oracles. He thought judgment had come; that punishment was actually falling on the guilty people, and that all the land would be laid desolate for ever. It was not so. The invasion came in sight, came close and then, it seems, turned aside. We have no record of exactly what happened, but it appears that Judah at any rate was not ravaged. Perhaps the Scythians kept to the coast and contented themselves with plundering the Philistines; perhaps they turned back to the north. We hear of no burnt cities or captives carried off; there was still time for repentance. It was well that there was time, for a few years later an event happened which was, as it turned out, of the very first importance.

In 621, the eighteenth year of Josiah, a book

[1] Isaiah v. 25–30.

was found in the temple by Hilkiah the Priest[1],
who was in charge of the repairs then going on
there; he showed it to Shaphan, the king's scribe,
who took it to the king. This book was the original
Deuteronomy, not so long as the book we now
have and without its concluding chapters, but
containing the exhortations to faithfulness, the
condemnation of idolatry and the law of the one
altar. The discovery of this book was the most
epoch-making event in the history of the Jewish
religion since the arrival of the Hebrews in
Canaan. As we have it to-day it consists of a collection of three addresses, supposed to have been
made by Moses on the borders of the promised
land, to which are added the story of Joshua's
appointment to succeed Moses and two poems.
Detailed study of the laws and exhortations must
convince us that they belong to the time not of
Moses but of Manasseh. Some scholars think that
the book was written in secret, hidden in the
temple and lost perhaps during the troubles of
Manasseh's reign, till Hilkiah found it; others
that Hilkiah himself knew of the concealment and
produced the book as a discovery in order to give
it the authority due to an ancient writing. If this

[1] This official, like his predecessors, is always spoken of as 'the
Priest,' except in three instances (II Kings xxii. 4, 8 and xxiii. 4)
where the title has been amended. The title 'High Priest' was
not used till after the Exile.

was so Hilkiah would not feel that he was doing anything wrong. The time cried aloud for a reformation, and in order to have any effect, it must be a drastic one. The High Places must be abolished more thoroughly than before, and the work must depend, not on the command of the King, but on the word of the Lord himself. Josiah was young and promised well; now was the time to strike, and to strike hard, so that the work might be done for good, and no unworthy successor of his be able to spoil it. The authors of Deuteronomy, whoever they were, saw the great need of the country and were resolute to meet it. To them indeed, it was the call of God that they heard, and the voice of Moses too. To say that their burning words were his was scarcely an image. Such words as those of chapters xiii or xxviii were surely not their own; it was the voice of Moses speaking the words of God.

They had reason afterwards to feel that the event justified them; not only Josiah, but the whole nation recognised the authority of the voice, and stern as the commands of the book were, it was possible to carry them out. The High Places were destroyed and we never hear of their restoration. To make sure that they never should be restored, the priests who had served them and whose interests and livelihood were bound up with them were commanded to come to Jerusalem, the one true, clean and abiding High Place, and were there formed into an inferior priestly order, the Levites, and set to do the menial work of the temple for the priests of Jerusalem. This measure no doubt caused cruel suffering, and the country priests, forbidden to exercise their calling, and smarting with resentment at being called idolaters, cried out, no doubt, against its injustice;—well, the faithful servant of the Lord must harden his heart; at all costs the guilt of idolatry must be purged away; these men, who had fallen into the very sins of the ancient Canaanites, must endure the same punishment as theirs. In actual fact the Canaanites had been subjugated, but never destroyed; they had been honourably employed by the king, and their rights respected by the prophets[1], but their worship remained as the type of corruption, therefore, in Deuteronomy, the true Israelite is told to destroy them all. In chapter xii, he is urged to the slaughter of the Canaanites; in chapter xiii it is one's own family, one's friend, brother or wife who is to perish; for the authors of the book saw Canaanites in all the worshippers of Ashtaroth, and the men who burnt their children to Moloch. This was certainly Josiah's view, he took the work of reform at once in hand, the High

[1] II Sam. xii. 1–15.

Places were destroyed and defiled and Topheth with them; the heathen altars in the Temple and in all Jerusalem were broken down and the Asherah and the vessels belonging to them burnt and beaten into dust; relics of the great days of the kingdom, monuments of Solomon's reign, which had escaped even Hezekiah and Isaiah, were thrown down and reduced to heaps. One altar only was left, the altar of Yahweh in the Temple, and to it was gathered the one priesthood. From all over the country, from Judah and as much of Northern Israel as recognised Josiah's authority, the priests came in. In one place, we are told that the country priests were killed on their altars[1], but if this was ever done, it can only have been in isolated instances, where there was some special act of resistance. To some, all this must have seemed an unwarranted and cruel novelty; to others, a righteous judgment and the sweeping away of iniquity; to some it was merely the command of the king, to others the word of the Lord. We naturally have only the account preserved by those who took the latter view, but we may be sure that the reformers would not carry their point without a struggle, which was, in fact, the judgment of friend and brother to which the book of Deuteronomy called them. We can see the

---

[1] II Kings xxiii. 20.

traces of this struggle in Kings and Ezekiel[1]. The arrangement became permanent and developed; in Deuteronomy and Jeremiah, we find the priests of Jerusalem and the country priests spoken of as one body, 'the priests, the Levites'; in later books, Ezekiel and Leviticus, they are more clearly distinguished as 'the Priests and the Levites[2].'

In this work of reformation, Jeremiah seems to have taken but a small part. With its object, the destruction of idolatry and the purification of worship, he must have been in complete sympathy; in the eleventh chapter, we see what he did to support it. He spoke both in Jerusalem and in the other cities, urging the people to hear the words of 'this Covenant' and to obey the voice of the Lord. His exhortation is to obedience in general; he says nothing in detail about the one altar or the one priesthood; nor do we find this teaching in any of his other oracles. It seems as though he had gone heartily with the reformers in all their ethical teaching, their demand for mercy and justice among neighbours, purity of worship and the love of God. And it appears that he also acquiesced in the necessity of bringing up the country priests to Jerusalem. He lived there

---

[1] II Kings xxiii. 9; Ezek. xliv. 10–13.
[2] Compare Deut. xviii. 1 and 6–8 with II Kings xxiii. 9 and Ezek. xliv. 6–16.

himself after this time, if he had not done so before. This may have been what turned his own family against him. To them he would appear as the traitor, who had surrendered their honour and yielded to the pretensions of the Zadokites. If Jeremiah was himself only half in sympathy with the Zadokite priests and felt that the going up to live in Jerusalem was only a needful expedient to ensure the utter demolition of the High Places, this accusation must have been peculiarly bitter to him; he in his turn looked on his kinsmen as traitors to a far higher interest than that of their family tradition. His call to the nation for obedience is followed by an outburst of pain and bitterness, as he speaks of the conspiracy in Anathoth against him, and of how nearly he fell a victim to it.

The oracles of this time are full of the sense of deep shame with which the prophet, as he grew up and looked about him, realised the sin of his countrymen. There are the warnings on the occasion of the Scythian raids, the call to return to the old path, the simpler ways of early times before the monarchy; the passionate protest against talking of peace, when there was no peace, which he often afterwards had to repeat; the call to accept the reformation which was the most available form for repentance to take.

FIRST PERIOD

626 TO 608 B.C.

FROM THE THIRTEENTH YEAR OF JOSIAH
TO HIS DEATH

i. 1–3	Baruch's introduction.
i. 4–10	Jeremiah's call.
i. 11–19	The almond rod and the seething cauldron.
ii. 1–3	Israel in the Wilderness.
ii. 4–28	,, ,, ,, Broken cisterns, the strange vine, the wild ass.
ii. 29–37	,, ,, ,, Smitten in vain, the forgetful bride.
iii. 1–5	The treacherous wife on the bare heights.
iii. 6–25	Backsliding Israel and treacherous Judah; the Ark to be forgotten.
iv. 1, 2	'If thou wilt return....'
iv. 3–18	'Break up your fallow ground....' Invasion from the north.
iv. 19–22	'My bowels, my bowels!' Invasion.
iv. 23–31	Chaos.
v. 1–9	The streets of Jerusalem.
v. 10–19	The invasion of 'an ancient nation from afar.'
v. 20–29	Jeremiah by the sea.
v. 30–31	'A wonderful and horrible thing....'
vi. 1–8	The invasion of shepherds.
vi. 9–15	The grape gatherers, 'Peace, peace!'
vi. 16–21	The old path.
vi. 22–30	Refuse silver. Terror on every side.
xi. 1–5	Preaching the Covenant to the people.
xi. 6–8	Preaching in the cities.
xi. 9–14	The conspiracy against the Lord.
xi. 18–23	The conspiracy against Jeremiah.
xii. 1–6	Running with the footmen.
(xvii. 19–27	The Sabbath—this is probably a later insertion.)

CHAPTER II

SECOND PERIOD 608–604 B.C.

JEHOAHAZ AND THE FIRST FOUR YEARS
OF JEHOIACHIM

THE death of Josiah fell on the people of Judah as a great calamity. For generations they had been involved in the long duel between Egypt and the successive empires of Mesopotamia. They themselves had originally come from Mesopotamia, but afterwards Egypt was their most important neighbour. Since the eighth century B.C., Assyria had been dominant, but now it was weakening, and in 608 Pharaoh Necho led an Egyptian expedition northwards to recover his lost Syrian provinces. Josiah marched against him to stop the way and was defeated and killed at Megiddo. We do not know Josiah's motive, he may have felt himself bound by his duty to his overlord to interfere, or, though not bound, he may have feared the change of masters. The prophets had always urged that the nation should keep out of the unending dispute; they must indeed expect to be made over according to the fortune of war, from one combatant to another, but it seems to have been the prophets' policy that they should accept such changes passively and be content with administering their internal affairs. Had Josiah lived and reigned as long as his grandfather, he might have preserved Judah as a self-governing state, though a dependent one; Jerusalem might not have been burnt, nor the people carried away to captivity in Babylon. When the Chaldeans succeeded the Assyrians and the Persians the Chaldeans, the people might have been less involved and less embittered. The teaching of 'the Second Isaiah' might have fallen on a kindlier soil, the long struggle inspired by Ezekiel, Nehemiah and Ezra against the Samaritans might have been less fierce. Struggle there had to be, subjection and poverty, but there might have been room for a true life, a natural dispersion by way of trade, such as is always open to poor countries, and Judah might have become the 'Servant of the Lord,' and a preacher to all nations, without being, as the Romans said of it, 'hostile to all men.' If Jeremiah thought thus of the possible future of his people, his hopes were to be disappointed. With Josiah an element of sanity and strength was gone, which his successors failed to renew, and in twenty-two years his throne had fallen, his city was burnt, his country in slavery.

Those twenty-two years were divided between

four reigns with a curious symmetry. Three of Josiah's sons and one of his grandsons followed him; twice over a reign of 'three months' (probably a phrase meaning 'a short time'), ending in exile, was followed by a reign of eleven years. First Jehoahaz reigned for three months, then Pharaoh Necho took him away and appointed his brother Eliakim, renamed Jehoiachim. We have a monument to Jehoahaz in Jeremiah's and Ezekiel's laments over him[1]. For four years Jehoiachim reigned as the vassal of Egypt; the prophets whose writings tell us of these years are Jeremiah, Nahum and Habakkuk.

Jeremiah went on with his preaching, as in the last reign, though he had lost a friend in Josiah, and gained an enemy in Jehoiachim. He never succeeded in gaining the ear of the whole people, but he had friends who protected his life and, in course of time, his books. He had to deal with two powerful parties, the princes and the priests; the princes were as yet fairly friendly to him, they were the patriots who put their country above everything; for them Judah was what Italy was to Mazzini or England to Nelson, something beyond criticism or question. They were ready to die for its liberty and independence, and for its religion too, because it was the national religion. The God

---

[1] Jer. xxii. 10–12; Ezek. xix. 1–4.

of their fathers was naturally their God; he was their king and their captain. The highest duty they knew was to fight for their country and their God; to speak of any duty to God which clashed with this seemed to them mere raving. Their vision of God was, in fact, a personification of the nation, its honour and liberty were his, a fallen state would mean a fallen God, to imagine which was treachery; but they probably saw that amendment of life was desirable in itself and for the good of the country, and they wished Jeremiah success. The attitude of the priestly party was much the same, only that, in its case, the idea of the nation reflected the idea of God, instead of the idea of God depending on the idea of the nation. It was his manifestation in the world; he was bound to it and could not forsake it. For his honour's sake God must always save Israel, as he had so often done, especially a hundred years earlier, when Sennacherib had besieged Jerusalem, and, in their own day too, from the Scythians. To them Jeremiah was not only a traitor, but a blasphemer as well. Moreover, though willing to help in bringing about the Deuteronomic reform, he had not been enthusiastic about it and they were the more turned against him by this want of complete agreement. The Temple was the centre of the Deuteronomic system but, in Jeremiah's teaching, the Temple and all its ordinances took at most a secondary place. Jeremiah's feeling towards his opponents was as vehement as theirs towards him and often as bitter; he believed that both princes and priests were leading the country and the foolish, ignorant mass of the people into disaster; his own life was one of 'perpetual pain'; there was one moment when he even felt that he must not pray for the people and this thought came to him, not as the revolt of his own mind from the suffering it could not bear, but as the command of the Lord. In spite of this, he still does pray and teach with unabated energy. He renounced marriage, because he would not bring up children to sorrow; it was perhaps not only marriage in general of which he was thinking when he wrote, but some particular marriage that he might not make. He felt that he had not been meant to be a man of strife with every man's hand against him; on the contrary, common life in homes and fields was dear to him; he liked farms, trees and birds, festivals and songs; he loved the cultivated hills. We can see, in his poems on a great drought, what kind of man he might have been if he had lived in less stormy times. The sea he did not care for, it seemed to him desolate and rebellious, something to be re-strained and kept away from the land that it threatened. At one moment of despair, he wishes that he might get away into the wilderness and be the keeper of a lonely inn where no one would stay for more than a night and where he might be free from all the entanglement of the city and its politics; it is the revulsion of a naturally social man. Actually, he never tried to escape, but lived on in Jerusalem preaching to a people that would not hear, telling them that God was a real person, not the shadow of themselves, or the projection of their own thoughts or likings, not bound by their wishes or their magic, and subject to no national law or religious ritual; that so long as they failed in known duties, so long as they oppressed the poor, or allowed false ideas of God to hide their own sins from them, nothing they could do would ever stand and they were bound to fall sooner or later. As their secular life grew and deepened, their thoughts about God had not grown and deepened with it; they were contented to keep their old childish ideal of a tribal God, one to be known by legends and approached by ceremonies, thinking as their fathers had thought in the old half-barbarous days, and so it happened that the very ideals of those older days, which might have been stepping-stones, had become idols. With Baal and Ashtaroth continually before their eyes, they could not think truly and they could not learn

to free themselves from the temptation to oppress
the poor, which must always increase as material
wealth increases and brings distinction of classes,
unless the knowledge of God grows with it, bringing reverence for all men as his creatures, and
making all distinctions only the means of a yet
fuller revelation of his infinite life. Jeremiah, too,
liked to look back, not with the instinctive desire
after magic, which we all inherit from our remote
ancestors, but with desire for what seemed a time of
innocence and simplicity. But he did not seriously
propose a return to the life of nomads; he liked to
draw pictures of it, but his desire for the people was
that they should dwell in the land and give up not
civilisation, but elaboration and luxury[1]. They
thought that because Yahweh had saved the nation
before, he would always keep it safe; Jeremiah
never thought so, and the history of the years from
the death of Josiah to the destruction of Jerusalem,
showed that he was right.

And after all this opposition and bitterness
between prophet and priest, it is to the priests that
we owe the preservation of Jeremiah's teaching.
His writings were preserved in the first instance
by Baruch and perhaps other friends, but later it
was the priests, the scribes and elders of the exiled
community in Babylon who kept the manuscripts,

[1] Jer. vii. 3, 7.

copied and edited them and taught their doctrine. The fiercest denunciations, the most passionate accusations against all that they held dear, were saved for us by the priests themselves. If they failed to recognise the prophets during their lives, the Jews certainly did it after their death.

In the beginning of Jehoiachim's reign, there was still hope that the nation as a whole might hear, and that the public situation might be saved. Thirteen years had passed since Josiah's reformation; the national worship was duly centralised and organised. Jeremiah now appealed to the people, not merely as citizens but also as individuals, urging every man among them to reform.

We read the account of this preaching in chapters vii, viii and ix with chapter xxvi. The former chapters give us the account of what Jeremiah said and the latter of the way his teaching was received. His address is given fully in chapter vii, less fully in chapter xxvi. In each we have the prediction that if the people will not repent, the Temple shall be left as desolate as Shiloh. It was this prediction that aroused the riot of which we read in chapter xxvi when the priests and the prophets would have put him to death, if the princes and the people had not prevented them. At this point it seems that Jeremiah finally parted company with the Deuteronomic reformers. He tells them that because of their evil life, because they steal, murder and commit adultery and worship other gods, therefore their faith in the Temple is a lie and God will destroy it. Nor is this all. Jeremiah does not merely say that their sins prevent them from receiving the blessings of the holy place, he says that they have misunderstood the true doctrine; the obedience that God asks for is not concerned with sacrifice. When God brought the people out of Egypt, he had no commands to give them about sacrifice. This passage is a very startling one and perplexing so long as we read the Bible without observing the order in time of the different books. But Jeremiah's teaching is quite plain, as well as the similar teaching of Amos, prophesying some sixty years before the fall of the Northern Kingdom as Jeremiah was now prophesying some twenty years before the fall of the Southern one[1]. When we recognise that the Pentateuch and the sacrificial law which it contained were the work of the exiles in Babylon who preserved the oldest traditions of the race, and added to them the religious laws of their own time, we can see how it was that to both Amos and Jeremiah the ordered ritual and elaborate sacrifices of their times appeared as a modern innovation. They seem to have taken sacrifice for granted, as

[1] Compare Jer. vii. 21–26 and Amos v. 25.

a thing that people would naturally do, but one which had very little connection with the deeper and truer knowledge of God which they and all the true prophets were teaching, a thing about which God would give no command and which he would readily abominate if it were not accompanied by a pure life. Jeremiah speaks of the Ark in much the same way as if the observance paid to it were a thing not exactly to be blamed but to be outgrown.

As we read chapters vii and viii, we see that the false worships cast out by Josiah have returned. Jeremiah refers to the burning of incense to Baal, the worship of the Queen of Heaven and the sacrifice of children to Moloch. He may possibly be looking back and recalling the sins of Manasseh's time, or of the early part of Josiah's reign, but it seems on the whole more probable that these worships would revive if not publicly yet privately, and that he is reproaching the people with what they are actually doing, not with the sins of a past time. It would be very difficult to stamp out a domestic rite carried on in private; we can see from later events how the women longed after the worship of the Queen of Heaven and it is not very likely that any law could prevent their burning incense to her in their own houses if they wanted to. In times of scarcity or drought such as we read about in chapters ix and xiv, the farmers would go back to the sanctuaries of Baal, the old god of the soil. Times of drought always make a peculiarly strong appeal for prayer; the rain comes we cannot see how, and it seems as if it must be so easy for some god to send it; a little offering of some sort would please Baal and could do no harm to Yahweh even if they were not one and the same. Even to-day country folk think no harm of spilling a little milk from the churn for the fairies and we find pleasure in relics of childishness like this, knowing that our best thought is but childish too, and that there is truth in childishness. Jeremiah does not deny it; he applies one test. Is the thing we do consistent with a good life? If a man lives at peace with his neighbour and believes that God is good, erroneous ideas about fairies will not do much harm; but once such ideas begin to lead him into wrongness of life or into low thoughts about God, he may follow them much further than he thinks, as the valley of the Son of Hinnom, close under the walls of Jerusalem, might bear witness.

One of the oracles of this time is difficult to date exactly, the discourse on Fishers and Hunters in chapter xvi. As it stands it consists of alternate promises and threats, and it is hard to see its exact application. The explanation may be that it was written as a threat of coming judgment and that in later years some scribe of the exile added the opening and closing verses, with the suggestion that the hunters sought out the people not to destroy them but to find and restore them to their country.

Another oracle, chapter xvii. 12–18, is somewhat difficult to follow, as the triumphant tone of the first two verses is not continued to the end; perhaps they were added later.

In the story of the Potter, we have one of the parables from daily life which Jeremiah saw so often. Watching the potter at his work, he drew the lesson which many others have drawn, and put it into words that many of them have quoted. The lesson is obvious enough, but that does not trouble Jeremiah. The lessons which his people were refusing to learn were, most of them, quite obvious; it was obviously no use to hope for peace while they allowed injustice, loose living and unworthy thoughts of God.

In chapter xviii there are three verses which some feel must be a later insertion. The prophet is speaking again of plots against his life. In verses 19, 20 he speaks with natural indignation of the ingratitude of the people he loved. In verses 21–23 he, or his editor, curses them with savage bitterness. It may be that Jeremiah, who was vehement and

by no means of an easy temper, might speak like
this in a moment of exasperation, but we can see
by his actions that it was not his permanent feeling
and it does not seem very likely that if he ever did
utter such words he would preserve them. Still,
it may be that he felt he was speaking about men
who were doing their utmost to destroy the last
hope of reform and salvation and that the awful
curses he invokes were not too harsh for his sense
of the crisis.

SECOND PERIOD

608–604 B.C.

JEHOAHAZ AND THE FIRST FOUR YEARS
OF JEHOIACHIM

CHAPTER III

THIRD PERIOD 604–597 B.C.

THE LAST SEVEN YEARS OF JEHOIACHIM

DURING all this time, Judah had been subject to Egypt, but in the fourth year of Jehoiachim, the Egyptian supremacy came to an end. A new power appeared in Mesopotamia, in the person of Nebuchadrezzar, the young king of Babylon, whose father, Nabopolassar, had rebelled against Nineveh and set himself up as an independent sovereign in the ancient city of Babylon on the lower Euphrates. Nebuchadrezzar had now no fear of Assyria, for Nineveh had fallen about the year 606. We have no details of the fall of Nineveh, though we see in Nahum's prophecy how the event impressed the Jews, but the older empire was out of the way and Nebuchadrezzar was already in its place to take up the quarrel between north and south. In the first year of his reign he marched west and after defeating the Egyptians at Carchemish, on the Euphrates, drove them back out of Syria into their own country. He did not at the moment pursue his advantage, but went away again. He had to make his dominion secure in his own country, and knew that Egypt was too thoroughly crushed to attempt any reprisals for the present. There followed a time of reprieve for the Jews; Assyria was gone; Egypt was gone; for three years Jehoiachim went on paying tribute to Nebuchadrezzar, but when he left off nothing happened and it seemed as if Babylon might be gone too[1]. The times were troubled and the country suffered from the attacks of its neighbours and hereditary enemies—bands of Syrians, Moabites, Ammonites and Chaldeans[2]; but the more awful danger of a regular invasion, with the threat of exile behind it, seemed to have withdrawn. With the two great thunderclouds of Egyptian and Mesopotamian domination dispersed, the Jews might well hope for the sunshine to return; those who had foretold disaster and captivity had been proved wrong, the Lord was among his people, he had saved them again and would still save them, so they trusted in him, even to the making of good pots out of faulty clay, and were not afraid.

It was the time of Jeremiah's deepest despair. It seemed impossible to find any appeal to touch the people, and yet with his whole heart he knew them to be wrong. 'This is my grief,' he said, 'and I must bear it.' In 604, the year of the

---

[1] II Kings xxiv. 1.   [2] *Ib.* xxiv. 2.

battle of Carchemish, he spoke an oracle in which
he summed up all his earlier teachings and assured
the people that Nebuchadrezzar was to bring the
punishment of their idolatry[1]. It would seem that
this oracle was spoken before the battle, when
Nebuchadrezzar was still advancing and Jeremiah
seems to have thought, as he did when the
Scythians were coming, that the blow was to fall
at once; a few weeks later, Nebuchadrezzar had
gone, after merely imposing tribute on Jerusalem
to mark its transference from the sway of Egypt
to his own. It must have seemed that Jeremiah
had yet again been a false prophet of evil. This
oracle, as we have it now, contains the famous
prediction that the captivity in Babylon would
last seventy years; Jeremiah's own words probably
end with verse 11: 'These nations shall serve the
king of Babylon seventy years'; the number
'seventy' standing like our own 'thousand' for a
great many. The next three verses seem to have
been added later by someone else who, in verse
13, refers to Jeremiah in the third person. This
writer is anxious to show that Jeremiah has been
justified by events; Jeremiah's own concern when
he spoke was not to justify himself or to chronicle
future events, but to exhort to repentance. As it
turned out the exile, from the first captivity to the

[1] Jer. xxv. 1 ff.

first return, only lasted fifty-nine years. From the fall of Jerusalem to the same date forty-eight.

In this same year, Jeremiah made his appeal in a new way. Nineteen years earlier Deuteronomy had been laid before Josiah in the form of a book, and now Jeremiah collected his teachings of the last twenty-two years and made them into a book. We do not know how the prophets preserved their oracles in the first instance. They may have kept written notes and when, as they often did, they spoke in poetry, this would be an additional security. At any rate, Jeremiah was able to recite his oracles to Baruch who wrote them down and then read them aloud to the crowd on a fast-day; the princes who were in the king's house, hearing of this, sent for him, and he read the collection through to them. More struck, perhaps, by hearing them all together than they had been by hearing each as it was spoken, or else moved by the anxiety of some of their number, the princes sent Jeremiah a message to tell him to hide and themselves took the book to the king. No doubt there were many among the princes who were alarmed at the appearance of Nebuchadrezzar and troubled too by the evils that troubled Jeremiah so much. The king, however, was of another mind. From the wording of the story it seems that he burnt the roll of parchment piece by piece, taking each portion as it was read to him and burning it as he listened to the next, not in a sudden access of rage, but in a cold passion of deliberate fury. The princes tried to dissuade him, but not very whole-heartedly, and the roll was burnt. Jeremiah and Baruch hid themselves and the collection was written out again and enlarged. This time the king was given no opportunity of destroying it and it survived to be the original document of the book of Jeremiah as we have it now, probably, roughly speaking, the first seven chapters.

Jehoiachim stood for patriotism, as he understood it. The fire was in his eyes the proper place for the vile suggestion that evil might fall on the Holy Land, the home of his race where Yahweh himself dwelt among them. In his oracle on this king, Jeremiah describes him as covetous, violent and oppressive; like Solomon, he built a palace and compelled his subjects to work on it for him. The prophet contrasts his government with that of his father Josiah greatly to his disadvantage. As regards his public policy, at this distance of time we can only judge it by its fruit; Josiah, even if the battle was a rash one, died fighting for his overlord to whom he had sworn loyalty; but Jehoiachim brought his country to the edge of disaster because he miscalculated the power and intentions of Nebuchadrezzar and thought he could afford to break his oath. The story of his end is obscure, Jeremiah foretells for him 'the burial of an ass'; in the book of Kings we are told that he 'slept with his fathers'; according to Chronicles, he died a captive in Babylon, whither he was carried the year before his son Jehoiachin. This story is probably the product of a later time when the chronicler wished to think that Jehoiachim had reaped the reward due to him along with his unhappy subjects; the book of Kings, which was compiled by his contemporaries, is more likely to be accurate[1].

In chapter xii we have another warning of the coming judgment, specially remarkable for its use of terrible images; the dearly beloved becomes an unclean bird, a wild beast, shepherds have destroyed the vineyard, what is sown as wheat comes up as thorns. For the prophet himself, we have renewed lamentations and the sense that not only man, but God, is against him.

Jeremiah put his teaching into two acted parables—the ruined girdle, and the broken bottle. The good clean linen of the girdle was soiled and rotted by the waters of the Euphrates; he bought it new and fresh, untouched from the hands of its maker—like Israel in her first innocence, thought the prophet as he carried it to the bank

[1] Jer. xxii. 19; II Kings xxiv. 6; II Chron. xxxvi. 5–8.

of the river, which he calls the Euphrates. It may
have been the Parah, near Anathoth, so called for
the occasion in order to point the moral. There he
buried the girdle in a hole, and the water, a type
of the Assyrian worship of Astarte, rotted it. The
symbol reminds us of the complaint of Juvenal
in a later age, that the Orontes had flowed into the
Tiber; certainly, in the days of Jehoiachim, the
Euphrates filled the Pool of Siloam.

The other foreign worship, that of Moloch,
was condemned in the breaking of an earthen
bottle in the valley of the Son of Hinnom. The
sanctuary of Topheth had been destroyed by
Josiah[1], but it seems now to have been built again.
Jeremiah speaks of the wickedness that went
on there with an energy that suggests that it was
not only a matter of shameful history. In the time
of its greatest prosperity, Topheth was no doubt
as magnificent a place as its votaries could make
it; its priests would naturally be anxious that it
should rival the Temple of Yahweh on the hill
above, where the same deity, said they, Melech,
the king, was worshipped with milder rites. The
name Molech, or Moloch, is a Hebrew adaptation
of the real name, Melech. 'Melech' means
'King'; 'Bosheth' means 'shame'; the Jews
changed the vowels of one word for those of the

[1] II Kings xxiii. 10.

other by way of a terse criticism. In the sanctuary of Molech, the central place would be occupied by the great image, sitting with outstretched hands, on which the children who were to 'pass through the fire' to the god were laid, after having been killed, and these outstretched hands, working by some sort of mechanism, sprang up and flung the body through the open jaws into the furnace which flamed inside, while music played to drown the screams of the victim under the knife, and the mother stood by with a glad face because of the honour done to her child. It is difficult for us to realise the state of mind in which parents could reconcile themselves to this sacrifice, but we know that they did so in many countries and it was at any rate the offering of the best they had to give. So long as the child is thought of as the absolute property of the father, or so long as the individual lives only in the tribe, and has no personal duties or rights, it may be argued that the family or the tribe has a right to give, and indeed is at times bound to give what is only a passing embodiment of its own being. The god, the tribe, and the individual member of the tribe share one life and the separated life offered in sacrifice goes back to the source that will strengthen them all; besides, what can be more acceptable to God than this gift of the best? Jeremiah did not argue the point;

he told the people that as they had burned their children so they should presently eat them in the hunger of the siege, and having spoken, he dashed his bottle on the ground so that it could never be mended again.

From Topheth he went up to the Temple and there repeated what he had just said, making no distinction between the crowds in the two places. The priest, Pashur, it seems cared less about the scene at Topheth than about the disturbance in the Temple; he had Jeremiah beaten and put in the stocks till the following day. The account of the scene is followed by Jeremiah's wild lamentation, and his reproaches against God, who had deceived him and thrust him into such straits. And yet, even in this, the bitterest of his complaints, he regains confidence at last.

Another acted parable was the trial of the Rechabites. The Rechabites lived as nomads, they built no houses and grew neither corn nor vines, but kept to the wilderness life that Jeremiah so loved to recall, not unlike our gipsies. The first time that we hear of them, is when Jonadab, the son of Rechab, helped Jehu in his massacre of the worshippers of Baal; from that time they had gone on with their half-wild life, wandering about with their flocks. Some time in the reign of Jehoiachim, the fear of Nebuchadrezzar drove them to Jeru-

salem, and they settled there for a time, probably
pitching their tents inside the city or outside, close
to the walls. This may have been towards the end
of the reign, perhaps when Nebuchadrezzar was
sending to demand the unpaid tribute. Jeremiah
sent for the heads of the tribe and entertained
them in the room of a friend in the Temple. If
this took place after the occasion when he stood
in the Temple stocks, it would show that he had
some influential friends even among the priestly
party. His offer of wine was, we should suppose,
formal, made merely in order to give occasion for
the blessing which followed their refusal. We have
a glimpse here of Jeremiah as a courteous host,
receiving his guests with kindness and dismissing
them with a blessing, not as he drew his own
portrait on another occasion, entertaining unknown
guests in a lonely khan, anxious only to escape
from human intercourse. But though the feast
may have been pleasant enough for the Rechabites, for their host it was sad. The lesson he drew
from it was again obvious; Jonadab, the son of
Rechab, had more honour from his descendants
than the Lord received from his people, who refused to amend their ways, and therefore could not
stay in the land that had been given them, but
would have to wander further than the homeless
Rechabites, not as once they did led in the Wilder-

ness by Yahweh, but to a land of exile and strange
gods. And for some of them the time had now
come.

THIRD PERIOD
604–597 B.C.

THE LAST SEVEN YEARS OF JEHOIACHIM

CHAPTER IV

FOURTH PERIOD 597–587 B.C.

THE REIGN OF ZEDEKIAH TILL THE SIEGE

IN 597 the blow fell which Jeremiah had so long foreseen. Nebuchadrezzar had made his empire safe in the east, and was free to turn his attention westwards. Jehoiachim had left his tribute unpaid for four years and Nebuchadrezzar determined to settle with him. Apparently Jehoiachim died just at this time and his son Jehoiachin was left to reap what he had sown. Jehoiachin had been on the throne only a few weeks, 'three months,' when Nebuchadrezzar's army appeared, followed by Nebuchadrezzar himself. Perhaps the Chaldean advance was sudden. At any rate there was, it seems, scarcely a struggle. The kingdom fell, the treasures were seized. Several thousand of the leading citizens with their families and the king himself were carried away into exile[1].

Jeremiah laments for the unhappy young king, as though the spectacle of the departure were actually before his eyes, as perhaps it was. Jehoiachin came with his mother out from the cedar palace

[1] II Kings xxiv. 8–17.

that his father had built 'in unrighteousness,' and went away with the enemy 'of whom he was afraid,' never to return. Zedekiah, his uncle, succeeded him; but his was only the shadow of a monarchy, and even so it did not last long. It was Jehoiachin who seems to have kept the affections of his people, even in his captivity, and when he died, still a captive, living on Nebuchadrezzar's alms, the royal line that had ruled in Judah for over four hundred years came to an end. The prophet Ezekiel was among the exiles; he, too, never saw Jerusalem again except in memory and vision, and, like Jeremiah, he lamented over the two young captive kings who died one in Egypt and one in Babylon in his poem on the two lion cubs[1].

The one hope for the country now lay in complete submission. Jeremiah was certain of this and urged it on all whom he could reach—the new king, the people and the envoys who came from other nations to congratulate Zedekiah on his accession. It was a strange time for compliments, but no doubt the envoys had other business in hand as well. All the countries of Western Asia were involved in the same catastrophe, and though they had of necessity submitted, yet they were all longing to make another stand for freedom. We

[1] Ezek. xix.

are not told what they thought of Jeremiah's advice. The king could not do much, he respected Jeremiah and consulted him at times when he dared, but was generally overruled by the princes. As for the people they would not and could not listen. They still clung to the conviction that the Lord was bound by his word and by his honour, he could not forsake them, he could not leave them unavenged. His city had been taken, his house robbed; even if he did not pity his people, he could not suffer himself to be so insulted, he would break out suddenly when the time was ripe; with one blow he would strike down the heathen king and overthrow his unrighteous empire. Was the arm of the Lord shortened that he could not save? They had not forgotten Gideon's barley cake or David and Goliath. The history of the Chosen People was full of stories of deliverance. Soon, quite soon, within two years at latest, the exiles would all be at home again and would bring the lost vessels of the Temple with them.

Jeremiah thought otherwise. He looked for no miracle except the one constant miracle of God's presence. After a time, he believed, the day would come for Chaldea too, it was unrighteous and no unrighteous nation can stand for ever; but, for the present, it was the Lord himself who had set Nebuchadrezzar over the nations, and they must submit. Jeremiah carried an actual wooden yoke on his shoulders, the sign of bondage and of submission; the prophet Hananiah could not bear the outward visible sign of the thing that in its invisible reality was burning every neck in Jerusalem; he took the yoke from Jeremiah and broke it, prophesying as he did so of restoration. Perhaps it was because Jeremiah longed so much that Hananiah might be right, that he did not answer at once, he said: 'Amen, the Lord do so,' but afterwards he knew that it could not be, and that to trust in a lie was still the last misfortune. There was yet punishment to bear and the more fully they accepted it, the sooner its work would be done. Hananiah's speech was from himself, not from the Lord; such speech is rebellion, and rebellion brings death to the rebel and destruction to those who listen to him.

After this time there is a change in Jeremiah's teaching. He sees a new vision and, for the first time, it carries a message of positive hope. As usual it came in a homely form, one that might be seen in any street where the fruit seller set out his wares for sale. There are two baskets of figs, and though the one basketful is bad and rotten, the other is good; never before did Jeremiah see any group of his countrymen as good. The good figs are the exiles who have been gathered into a

separate basket, not to be thrown away, but for
use. It was not Nebuchadrezzar who had carried
them off to serve his own ends, but the Lord, who
had sent them into exile because he had a purpose
for them, which was to be fulfilled through it. The
exiles already perceived, through the witness of
their own consciences, that they had not gone so
far away as to be beyond the reach of the presence
of God; this had always been one of the terrors of
exile to them and now they found by experience
that it was an illusion. They began to think that
their God was not simply another national god,
like Assur, Bel and the rest, only less powerful
because he had been defeated by them; this would
have been the case had he been like their idea of
him; but it was not so. His fortunes did not rise
and fall with the fortunes of his people, the power
of Nebuchadrezzar could not hurt him; in fact,
consciously or not, Nebuchadrezzar was his servant, doing his work, and so the loss of the very
thing that had seemed to be the indispensable
revelation, the Holy City and the Temple, became
the means of a greater revelation. They were, in
fact, beginning to realise the implications of what
they already believed, but had not understood so
well before, and though they were still too sore to
feel it, the new thought of God contained far
greater possibilities than the old. For Jeremiah

too there was a new hope; what the people now guessed, he had always known, but now at last he saw the truer vision spread among them. After this we have no more lamentations for himself; he does not again curse the day he was born or the friends who had betrayed him. He wrote to the exiles and advised them to be patient; to give up thinking about an early return; to make themselves at home in the land of captivity. They followed his advice, reconciled themselves to facts and settled in Babylon, living the life there which they might otherwise have lived in Jerusalem. Afterwards, when the way was open for a return, many of them stayed on, and became the ancestors of the Dispersion which played so important a part in later Jewish history.

But for the remnant in Jerusalem, there was as yet no such hope, they still went on in the old way, adding sin to sin. In chapter xxiii we have a series of pictures of the false king, the false prophets and false priests, and, as a contrast, of the true king who should surely come some day, whom Jeremiah and others after him called the Branch and whose name is 'the Lord our righteousness.' This name is the translation of the name Zedekiah and what seems to be meant is that while the branch of the stem of David is to be the true Zedekiah, the false shepherd of the preceding verses is the shadowy Zedekiah, who sat so insecurely on the throne of his fathers and his nephew; if so, we have a poem on each of the last four kings. The false prophets are the greatest sinners of all in Jeremiah's eyes; for those who profess to lead the flock and can only lead it astray, who run when they are not sent and use conventional phrases to pass off their own thoughts and wishes as the oracles of God, he has nothing but wrath and scorn.

In chapters xxx and xxxi we have a collection of prophecies that speak of hope. These two chapters lie like a ray of sunlight across the stormy scene of Jeremiah's life. Taking them as a whole, they are inspired by the thought of the new hopes opening before the exiles; the prospect of return, the promise of restored health, of God's unfailing love, of consolation and blessings and the new covenant to be given by God. These prophecies do not all belong to the period we are now considering; one passage reminds us of an exilic writing in the book of Isaiah[1]; another recalls one of the prophecies of Jeremiah's youth[2]; a later phrase suggests Ezekiel's teaching[3], parts were certainly written after Jerusalem had been

---

[1] Jer. xxxi. 1–9. Comp. Isaiah xxxv.
[2] Jer. xxxi. 20, 22. Comp. iii. 19, ii. 1–3, iii. 12.
[3] Jer. xxxi. 29, 30. Comp. Ezek. xviii. 2–4.

burnt[1]. It seems as if the two chapters were composed of many oracles made at various times and by various writers and put together to show what Jeremiah's hopes, when he expressed them, were. The whole group may at one time have formed the conclusion of the book of his writings. In the book as we read it now, there are three collections of oracles interspersed with chapters consisting of narrative matter, probably by Baruch; chapters i–xxv are a collection of oracles from all periods of the prophet's life; xlvi–li are the oracles on foreign nations, and we have besides these two chapters which are entirely hopeful. It may be that at one time these three groups formed the whole book and that the hopeful prophecies were put at the end and that then Baruch's narrative was introduced and this order was changed. In the Septuagint, the Greek translation of the Old Testament, we have yet another arrangement. The chief feature of the group is the oracle about the new covenant in chapter xxxi. This passage gives its own character to the whole two chapters, and interprets all Jeremiah's teaching; and this we may take as Jeremiah's own, though its authenticity has not gone wholly unquestioned. It tells of what is to come for those who have learnt the lessons of captivity and exile; in it Jeremiah fore-

[1] Jer. xxx. 18, xxxi. 4.

sees the whole nation as having done with shadows and become capable of a true spiritual worship. The Temple and the sacrifice disappear, and each man stands in an individual relation to God with his sin forgiven and his ruin restored.

FOURTH PERIOD
597–587 B.C.
THE REIGN OF ZEDEKIAH TILL THE SIEGE

CHAPTER V

FIFTH PERIOD 587–586 B.C.

THE SIEGE AND FALL OF JERUSALEM

ZEDEKIAH reigned for eleven years, and during nine of those years the good figs ripened and the bad figs rotted. The exiles followed Jeremiah's advice, settled and, in many instances, became wealthy. They had leisure for reflection and for literature, and it is to them that we are indebted for our possession of their scriptures. Had the exiles been involved in the struggle for a living and in political excitement, as the remnant at home were, we might never have had the Old Testament, for it was during the exile that the various books already written were arranged, edited and copied in such numbers as secured their survival. The single volume which we can now take from our shelves and hold in one hand is the direct descendant of the long parchment scrolls which were the work of the scribes of the exiles. The promise made to Abraham that his descendants should be as the sand of the sea for number, has certainly come true for the document in which it is recorded.

The congregational gatherings that met to hear the reading of these scriptures and for prayer were another fruit of the exile, and they too have borne their fruit all the world over. There were changes in the thought as well as in the practice of the exiles; they learnt not only to hate but to despise the idolatry that had ruined their country; what had been a temptation to them in their own country was now a sign of bondage and, moreover, a senseless vanity. Baal, Ashtaroth and Molech in Judah might be accounted for as particular forms of Yahweh, but on a foreign soil and in exile, these forms shrivelled up and vanished because they had not the one quality that was now seen to be Yahweh's essential characteristic; they spoke of the vital impulse which keeps the world and all creatures in existence, and this did indeed belong to the revelation of God, all life came from him and all the good things of life were his gift; but the fact of his righteousness was more important and for the mass of the people this knowledge was new. This new belief made any suggestion of evil in their thought of him, or even any suggestion of the unmoral indifference of the powers of nature, an impossible blasphemy, and the Chaldean ideas of the divine nature, whether expressed in images of wood and stone or in mental conceptions, became repulsive and ridiculous.

Learning to know God through his goodness, that is through his personal character, the Jews learnt, after a time, to recognise his presence among some of their new neighbours and to wish that they too might know him, not as a foreign conqueror coming to justify and deliver his chosen people and to overthrow the rest, but as the great and good king of all men. This was never altogether the dominant feeling among them, but it was present.

So in Babylon Jewish life was conquering new regions and showing itself in new forms, but not in Jerusalem. Zedekiah still 'did evil,' the old sins were unchecked, there was no force in the country to build up anything fresh. There was vain hope, vain talk of peace, at last foolish, hopeless rebellion. Zedekiah plotted with Egypt, and broke the oath that he had given to Nebuchadrezzar; the exiles felt the disgrace of the broken oath and the bitterness of looking on helpless while their country destroyed itself[1]; Jeremiah was in despair, he knew the country could not stand alone and that Egypt could not save it and he felt this constant intriguing to be treachery to the Lord; if God had not given the Jews sovereign dominion, why should they be so anxious to get it? He had given them a far better gift, the know-

[1] II Kings xxiv. 20 and Ezek. xvii. 15–20 and xxii.

ledge of himself, and this they despised; in order to make that gift their own they must amend their lives, but this they refused to understand and still chose to struggle after an impossible independence. From this time, Jeremiah's thought is not how the nation may be saved, but only individuals. Nebuchadrezzar had given the country a severe lesson in 597, and would no doubt have been glad if it had been enough and if he could have left Judah to settle its own internal affairs and to become a prosperous province of the empire, but now Zedekiah began to contrive fresh schemes with his arch enemy, not because he had any love for Egypt, but in the hope of playing it off against Chaldea. As the Samaritans long afterwards said to Artaxerxes, Jerusalem was a rebellious city, hurtful to kings and provinces[1], and it held the gate between north and south, therefore Nebuchadrezzar resolved, since he could not quiet it, to destroy it. The sequence of events, as they concern Jeremiah, is rather difficult to follow.

In 587 Nebuchadrezzar's army marched westwards, and while it was on its way, Zedekiah sent for Jeremiah and asked him to enquire of the Lord for the country. Perhaps he still hoped for a repetition of Isaiah's answer to Hezekiah but if so, he was disappointed, he only got the answer that

[1] Ezra iv. 15.

the Lord would 'gather the Chaldeans into the
midst of the city,' and would himself fight against
it. In addition to his reply to the king, Jeremiah
addressed an oracle to the people, recommending
them, in so many words, to surrender to the Chaldeans. He then went to the palace, with one more
appeal to the king. He brought a message from
the Lord, the city would be destroyed, but Zedekiah
should die in peace and receive the decent burial
which meant so much among all ancient peoples.
The promise of a peaceful end can hardly be said
to have been fulfilled, and the whole passage looks
as if some words had dropped out which showed
that it depended on Zedekiah's consenting to
yield before it was too late. Zedekiah was readier
to listen than Jehoiachim had been and made some
attempt to meet the prophet's demand; it was
about this time that he called upon his nobles to
release their Hebrew slaves and they did so.

The Chaldeans arrived and began the siege, but
the Egyptians went so far to redeem their promises
as to send an army to the help of Zedekiah, and
Nebuchadrezzar left Jerusalem and marched away
to meet it. The relief must have been enormous,
the people saw the army go, the cloud of dust
that marked its line of march fading away in the
distance, the dreaded 'mounts' that threatened

their wall, abandoned; surely they might well thank God and take courage, turning to the words of psalmists and prophets to find appropriate songs of thanksgiving for their deliverance[1]. To Jeremiah, these intervals of vain hope were peculiarly trying; he could not bear to see the people strengthening themselves in the determination not to surrender, and in the belief that they understood the counsel of God, while they would not repent. The nobles' first act, as soon as the danger seemed less, was to reclaim their slaves; Zedekiah sent again to ask for his prayers, and Jeremiah answered that even if the king had defeated the whole Chaldean army (instead of merely watching it go) yet the wounded men in it would rise up and take Jerusalem.

The enemy soon came back, but the short respite gave Jeremiah an opportunity to attend to his personal affairs. It seems that his father, or the head of his family, must have died at this time and he was wanted to take possession of his share of the inheritance. He set off to go to Anathoth for this purpose, and was arrested as he was passing through the gate, accused of 'falling away' to the Chaldeans, taken to the princes and by them imprisoned. We have two accounts of this

[1] Perhaps Isaiah xxxiii or Psalms xlvi and xlviii.

event, one in chapter xxxvii, which describes his arrest and imprisonment, the other in chapter xxxviii, which dwells on the anxiety of the princes, and tells how he was thrown into an old cistern, where he was in danger of sinking in the wet mud, but was rescued, with the king's permission, by one of his friends, Ebed-Melech, and the dungeon exchanged for an ordinary prison. It was a foreigner who rescued him and one who bore the name of Molech! The arrest shows how acute the divisions in the city had come to be; Jeremiah's friends felt that he, a man of high character and known purity of life, had been imprisoned on a false charge and nearly murdered; the princes, on the contrary, felt that a man who claimed to be a prophet and yet advised surrender, had shown himself to be an impostor, and worthy of death. Theirs was indeed a desperate task, they held on to the last, hoping for a miracle, staking everything on their religion as they understood it, or on their love of country; and here was Jeremiah throwing all his influence into the enemy's scale; however, at any rate he was now in prison, and there they kept him.

Once more the king sent for him and they met, as it seems, for the last time, in one of the gateways of the Temple. At a time like this a gateway might be a very suitable place for a secret meeting, as both parties could get there without attracting much attention, and there would be some little room at the side where they could talk without being overheard. Perhaps Zedekiah felt himself insecure in his own house, but no one could object if he went out of it to the Temple, and stayed a few minutes in the entry on his way. Zedekiah asked, 'Is there any word from the Lord?' Jeremiah repeated what he had already said so often, he had foretold judgment, and now it was here; the king and the people had listened to false prophets whose falsehood they ought to have perceived, and where were those prophets now? All that remained was to save individual lives and the city; if the king would give himself up, this might be done. Zedekiah could not bear the thought that he would be mocked by the Jews already in the Chaldean camp; Jeremiah pleaded in vain, the useless conversation came to an end, and they parted. The siege dragged on a little longer.

But siege or no siege, life goes on, and men have their private business to see to, even when the state is falling. Jeremiah had been prevented from going to Anathoth and his family had carried out the division of the property without him. There was a certain field which now belonged to his uncle, who, not unnaturally, felt that he would prefer its value in money; the first refusal belonged, by right, to Jeremiah, would he care to use it? The question must have seemed almost farcical at first, as questions of every-day life do in the middle of a great tragedy; but to Jeremiah's uncle it was serious enough, he had ruin before him and most likely exile, seventeen shekels might be of considerable use; to Jeremiah the offer gave an opportunity for his last sermon to the nation before its fall, and that sermon was to be a lesson of hope.

His uncle did not want the field. Well, he did. He too was in sight of exile and was already in prison, he had only just escaped death and might easily meet it at any moment; the field was in the country occupied by the enemy; this was the moment for him to buy and pay for it with all the proper formalities of which he, or Baruch, gives us the account. The story is told at full length in two chapters, with Jeremiah's prayer, and the answer, which recapitulates all the teaching of Jeremiah's ministry, and then passes into promises of restoration, of the new everlasting covenant, a converted heart and a reclaimed land. For the second time, Jeremiah was able to declare the positive side of his doctrine, to speak openly of the hope that made the burden of his life tolerable; he had done so once before when the presence of God showed itself among the exiles, and he saw the firstfruits of the new covenant beginning to ripen among them, and the voice which had spoken all his life in his heart denouncing sin, compromises and lies, spoke again of hope and restoration. As God was faithful, present with the exiles in the land of captivity, so he was faithful, present with the remnant even in their day of judgment in the sinful and falling city. He would work no wonder to turn away the punishment they had brought on themselves, but the fact of his presence showed that some day he would restore all that had been lost.

The story of the siege and of the purchase of the field suffers more than any other part of the history from the disarrangement of the chapters. It is given in chapters xxi, xxxiv, xxxvii, xxxviii, xxxii, xxxiii, xxxviii and xxxix; as it stands the first message from Zedekiah leads up to the collection of poems on the four kings; Jeremiah's message to the king precedes the story of the Rechabites and of the burning of the roll, and the story of the field precedes that. We cannot realise the force of the prophet's action unless we read the whole story in its right order.

FIFTH PERIOD
587–586 B.C.

THE SIEGE AND FALL OF JERUSALEM

CHAPTER VI

SIXTH PERIOD 586 B.C. AND AFTER

THE FLIGHT TO EGYPT

JERUSALEM fell, and all came about as Jeremiah had foreseen; city and Temple were burnt, and everything of any value that had been left before was carried off; the king was taken prisoner as he was trying to escape and the last thing he saw before his eyes were put out was the death of his sons. The people were collected, and all who were of any position or education were taken to Babylon, except a few refugees who escaped capture and those who were left to keep some sort of order in the ruined country. Jeremiah went with the others in chains, as far as Ramah, where Rachel 'wept for her children' from her tomb, but at this point his chains were taken off, and he was given his choice whether to go or stay. He chose to stay, was allowed to keep Baruch with him, treated with courtesy and supplied with food and money. A native governor had been appointed, Gedaliah, whose family had long been friends of Jeremiah; his grandfather, Shaphan the scribe, had been the first to whom Hilkiah the priest had shown the book of Deuteronomy on its discovery; his father, Ahikam, had saved Jeremiah's life in the first riot in the Temple[1].

Gedaliah settled at Mizpah, four or five miles to the north-west of Jerusalem. He may have felt that Jerusalem itself was too utterly dreary to live in; a little town, out in the open country, was less desolate, and safer too, than the larger city where footpads and robbers could hide among the ruins and prey on their fellows in misfortune. Jeremiah and other refugees joined him, some of the people who had been left to cultivate the land (for though the Chaldeans burnt the towns of their enemies, they did not destroy the crops or trees), and also some of the ladies of the royal family. Gedaliah did what he could to encourage the people, he set them to work at once on getting in the harvest; for two or three months nothing happened to disturb the refugees and it seemed as if they might at least look forward to a time of quiet, though of subjection and poverty, but it was not to be. There were still armed men, the remains of Zedekiah's army, at liberty in the country, and one of these, Ishmael, who had been one of the king's chief officers, and who was his relation, probably one of the princes with whom Jeremiah had had so many struggles, plotted with the king of Ammon. He

[1] II Kings xxii. 3, 12 and Jer. xxvi. 24.

still cherished the idea of escaping from the Chaldeans and hoped to set himself up somewhere under the protection of the Ammonite king, a strange dream for a Jew. He came with a band of ten men to Gedaliah, and was hospitably received; he then suddenly turned on his host, murdered him, his attendants, and the Chaldeans who were also there. Two days later he entrapped and murdered seventy out of eighty men who were on their way to Jerusalem, going to worship in the ruined Temple. How he was able to commit so many murders with so few companions is not very clear, but he took his victims by surprise and when they were in no mood for fighting. It is not clear either why he murdered the men who were going to Jerusalem, he may have hoped that they would join him, and when he found they would not, then have murdered them. At any rate, after this exploit he fled, carrying with him the women, who were perhaps destined to be the wives of his robber band, and Jeremiah. He may have thought that the presence of a holy man would bring a blessing with it. Another of the captains, Johanan, a friend of Gedaliah, who had already warned him in vain, collected all the fighting men he could get and followed Ishmael, caught him up and recovered the captives; but Ishmael himself, with eight companions, escaped and went to find such liberty as he could in the land of Ammon. Johanan now took command, but he was afraid to go back to Mizpah, lest the Chaldeans should be inclined to exact a penalty for the murders without enquiring too closely where the guilt lay. His thoughts turned towards Egypt, and he took his party of refugees southwards to Geruth Chimham, near Bethlehem, the destined home of the Deliverer promised long ago by Micah, who had never come to be the peace of his people against the invader from the north and to make them like the lion among the beasts of the forest[1].

At Geruth Chimham, the refugees halted to decide on what they were to do. The last hope of any sort of normal life in their own country seemed to be gone with Gedaliah; they stood between the Chaldeans and the robbers, the Lord had rejected them and home was home no longer. If only they could go right away, and never see the burnt houses and the deserted fields again! If they could go somewhere where they could forget, and be out of reach of those terrible armies that might return at any moment and against which they had no longer even the shadow of any protection! How safe and green the land of Egypt lay, with its fertile fields and rich cities and its unbroken armies, strong enough for defence still,

[1] Micah v. 2–9.

even though not for attack; could they not go there?

They consulted Jeremiah, and he did not answer at once. Perhaps he doubted, perhaps he felt that after all the horrors he had just gone through, he must have time before he could give them the answer that should be from the Lord and not from himself; for ten days he was silent, while the people sat on the hills and saw the heavens closed, and heard no angelic message, other than what he should give them.

When Jeremiah spoke at last, he spoke to them all together and he told them to stay. If they would stay, he said, there should be no need for fear, the Chaldeans should not hurt them; but if they went to Egypt, all the things they feared at home would follow them there, and they would never come back. They had given a promise beforehand to do whatever he told them, but they deceived themselves more than him when they made it, for they meant to go, and only wanted him to say they were right. Jeremiah's speech is like a repetition of the great exhortation at the end of Deuteronomy[1]. Never had he spoken more earnestly in the days when the nation and the Temple were there to be saved, than he did now, when it was only a question of 'the lowest of the

[1] Deut. xxviii.

people.' At first it is perplexing to see why he attaches so much importance to the matter; why should they not go, at least for a time, and wait in a place of safety till better days should perhaps come? If God could be with the exiles in Babylon, why not with the refugees in Egypt?

If this argument occurred to Jeremiah, he rejected it, the positions were different; these men had the choice, they were not forcibly carried off, for them flight would be running away from punishment, it would be putting their trust in Egypt as they had so often done, and never without suffering for it. To stay in Judah was to prove their trust in God; so long as they kept their hold on the land, they were claiming the fulfilment of the promises, and confessing their belief that God had a purpose for them. Flight was yielding to despair, and Jeremiah preached, not despair, but judgment and hope; he had spent his life in fighting the false hopes of his people, and now those false hopes had failed and Jeremiah assures them that what is left is of infinite value, that fragment of a task that still remained for them to do was worth all kinds of endurance and suffering to fulfil. Like the Sybil, who offered three books for the price that might have bought nine, Jeremiah counts the action of this remnant as having the value that the action of the whole nation might once have had.

Their hope is in the character of God, expressed
in his recognised purpose and there is no limit to
the good that Jeremiah foresees if the people will
accept that hope, even now. They had known
Yahweh as 'Yahweh of Battles,' 'the Lord mighty
in battle,' they had just had a lesson that God did
not mean to be known fully in that way; if that
was the whole of their knowledge, it was false. In
the eyes of the Egyptians and Chaldeans, Yahweh
was beaten and discredited, but for those who knew
him as the source of righteousness, it was not so;
because his people had sinned and all the more
because they were his people, he had given them
over to punishment; if they would repent and trust
in him, even a very few of them with nothing to
offer, they would find him as strong, as glorious
and as near as he had ever been, yes, and far
nearer than in the days when they brought vain
oblations and made his house a den of robbers.
Let them show their trust by living quietly in the
land where their lot had fallen, either in Babylon
or in Judah; God would save them in his own
time.

However, though Jeremiah preached hope, the
people chose despair, they fled and took him with
them, or else he chose to go when he saw he could
not keep them. The last thing we are told of him
is the story of his protest against the renewed

worship of the Queen of Heaven in Tahpanhes. And so he died, with nothing to show for his life's work except the fact that he and Baruch, and perhaps a few others had been true to the end. So far as we know, he had not the great comfort that comes from a belief in a better life to come, it was not the belief of the Jews in his time, a Jew who wanted to see God must see him in this life, he would never have a clearer vision; the other world, even for good men, was a place of darkness and dust, where there was neither knowledge nor strength[1].

But in the ruin of all his world, Jeremiah did see God; he recognised his action and heard his voice; he was sure that God had a purpose, which he himself could serve and that it was worth while to fight to the last to rescue even the least fragment that might help. And after all, events justified his hope. The future lay, not with the Jews in Egypt, who gave up hope, but with those in Babylon who held to it. After his death they began to understand the meaning, not only of his teaching, but of his life; to one among them, his figure blended with the figure of the ideal Israel, and took shape in the most wonderful vision of the Old Testament, and the most characteristic achievement of

---

[1] Psalms lxxxviii. 10–12, cxv. 17; Isa. xxxviii. 18, 19, etc.

Jewish thought, the Servant of the Lord[1], who saves his people, and all peoples, by bearing their sins and suffering for them. Among all the ideal figures that men have honoured, the Servant is peculiar in this, that he suffers deliberately, not only for the sorrow, but also for the sin of men, and this, not to find a way of escape, but for the sake of a positive joy to come through suffering. The Servant of the Lord cannot be described in any words except the words in which he is described in the book of Isaiah, and we must read that book if we are to know what was the lesson and the hope of Jeremiah's life. That hope came true. Looking back now on the history of the Jews and their religion, we see it strewn with error and failure in both thought and life; but only as the background to a great success. We only heed or remember the failures of the Jews because our attention is held by the great attainment which Jeremiah foresaw.

[1] Isa. xli. 8–20, xlii. 1–9, xliv. 1–5, xlix. 1–13, l. 4–9, lii. 13–liii. 12.

SIXTH PERIOD

586 B.C. AND AFTER

THE FLIGHT TO EGYPT

THE VARIOUS ORACLES OF THE BOOK
OF JEREMIAH AS MARKED BY THE
PARAGRAPHS IN THE REVISED VERSION
WITH THE NUMBERS OF THE PERIODS
UNDER WHICH THEY WILL BE FOUND

Printed in the United States
By Bookmasters